Salem Witch Trials

Colonial Life

Sean Price

Chicago, Illinois

RAINTREE

TO ORDER:
☎ Phone Customer Service **888-454-2279**
💻 Visit **www.heinemannraintree.com** to browse our catalog and order online.

Editorial: Adam Miller
Design: Ryan Frieson, Kimberly R. Miracle, and Betsy Wernert
Photo Research: Tracy Cummins and Tracey Engel
Production: Victoria Fitzgerald

Originated by DOT Gradations Ltd.
Printed and bound in the United States of America, North Mankato, MN

ISBN-13: 978-1-4109-3116-0 (hc)
ISBN-10: 1-4109-3116-1 (hc)
ISBN-13: 978-1-4109-3125-2 (pb)
ISBN-10: 1-4109-3125-0 (pb)

13 12 11
10 9 8 7 6 5 4 3 2

Library of Congress Cataloging-in-Publication Data
Price, Sean.
  Salem witch trials : colonial life / Sean Price.
    p. cm. -- (American history through primary sources)
  Includes bibliographical references and index.
ISBN 978-1-4109-3116-0 (hc) --
ISBN 978-1-4109-3125-2 (pb)
1. Trials (Witchcraft)--Massachusetts--Salem--Juvenile literature. 2. Witchcraft--Massachusetts--Salem--History--Juvenile literature. 3. Salem
(Mass.)--History--17th century--Juvenile literature. I. Title.
  KFM2478.8.W5P75 2008
  133.4'3097445--dc22
                                        2008011297
062011
006223RP

Acknowledgments
The author and publisher are grateful to the following for permission to reproduced copyright material: ©Alamy **pp. 24** (Old Paper Studios), **28** (Joe Devenney); ©AP **p. 29** (Wide World Photos); ©Boston Public Library **p. 15**; ©The Bridgeman Art Library **pp. 13** (Massachusetts Historical Society, Boston, MA), **4, 16, 18, 25** (Peabody Essex Museum, Salem, MA; ©Corbis **p. 22** (Bettmann); ©Courtesy Danvers Archival Center **p. 19**; ©Getty Images/ Time Life Pictures **p. 17** (Nina Leen); ©The Granger Collection, New York **pp. 7-R, 7-L, 14, 23, 26**; ©Henry W. Rutkowski/Rebecca Nurse Homestead **p. 12**; ©Jim McAllister **p. 10**; ©Library of Congress Geography and Map Division **p. 5**; ©Courtesy of Massachusetts Archives **p. 21**; ©Courtesy of the Massachusetts Historical Society **p. 27**; ©North Wind Picture Archives **p. 6**; ©Richard B. Trask **p. 11**; ©Courtesy, Winterthur Museum **p. 9**.

Cover image of The Examination of a Witch, 1853, by Tompkins Harrison Matteson, is used with permission of ©The Bridgeman Art Library/Peabody Essex Museum, Salem, Massachusetts.

The publishers would like to thank Consultant Name for her assistance in the preparation of this book.

Contents

Some words are printed in bold, **like this**. You can find out what they mean on page 30. You can also look in the box at the bottom of the page where they first appear.

Salem in 1692

In the 1690s, Salem was a small town. It was in Massachusetts. Massachusetts was not a state. It was an English **colony**. That meant the country of England sent people to live there.

Salem could be a tough place to live. Attacks by Native Americans took place. Bears and wolves lived in the woods. Men wore swords around town. Many people lived on farms. Salem was next to the Atlantic Ocean. Many people in Salem built ships for a living.

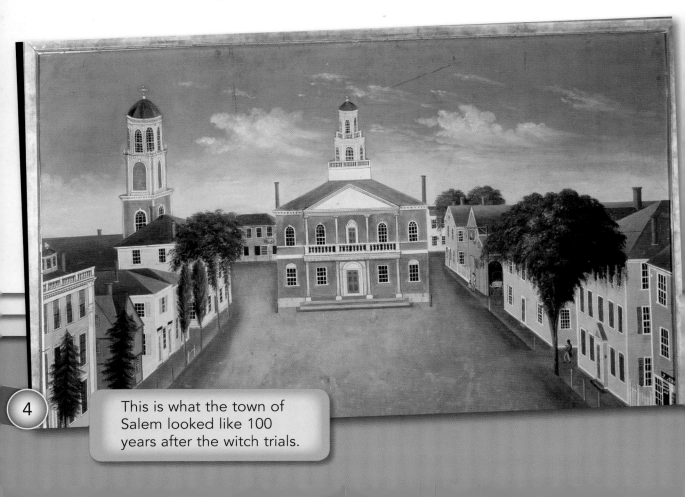

This is what the town of Salem looked like 100 years after the witch trials.

Most people back then believed in **witches**. These were women who helped the Devil. People believed that witches used evil powers to hurt others. In 1692, people in Salem saw strange things happening. They blamed it on witches. They began a hunt for witches.

This witch hunt was a terrible mistake. It caused the deaths of 25 people. None of them had done anything wrong.

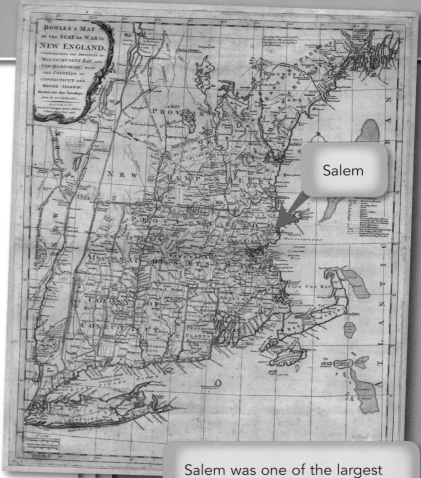

Salem

Salem was one of the largest towns in Massachusetts in the 1600s. The largest was Boston.

Male witches

Men accused of witchcraft were called wizards. Back then, being called a wizard was a terrible insult. Someone who was accused of being a wizard might be killed.

witch female who gets evil powers from helping the Devil

Family Life in Salem

Families were strict with their children in Salem. However, most parents were also loving to their kids.

Children went to work at a young age. Their families needed help. Families often owned farms. Sons helped their fathers in the fields. Many boys went hunting by age eight. They were expected to bring home food.

A boy dressed in a white shirt with wool pants. Boys' clothes were usually made of dark colors like green or black. These colors helped to hide them from animals or Indians in the woods. Boys also wore leather boots or moccasins.

Children in Salem learned to read. Some were taught using the Bible. Others used this picture book. It was called the *New England Primer*.

Mather was also a writer. He wrote a book about the trials. He wrote this book during the Salem witch trials. He hoped it would make people agree with the trials.

The Wonders of the Invisible World:

Being an Account of the

TRYALS

OF

Several Witches,

Lately Excuted in

NEW-ENGLAND:

And of several remarkable Curiosities therein Occurring.

Together with,

I. Observations upon the Nature, the Number, and the Operations of the Devils.
II. A short Narrative of a late outrage committed by a knot of Witches in Swede-Land, very much resembling, and so far explaining, that under which New-England has laboured.
III. Some Councels directing a due Improvement of the Terrible things lately done by the unusual and amazing Range of Evil-Spirits in New-England.
IV. A brief Discourse upon those Temptations which are the more ordinary Devices of Satan.

By COTTON MATHER.

Published by the Special Command of his EXCELLENCY the Governour of the Province of the Massachusetts-Bay in New-England.

Printed first, at Boston in New-England; and Reprinted at London, for John Dunton, at the Raven in the Poultrey. 1693.

Cotton Mather was a famous Massachusetts minister. He was also friends with men who would judge those accused of witchcraft. Mather told people to be tough against those accused of being witches.

Most towns could not pay for a school. Boys and girls learned from their parents. Kids learned to read using the **Bible**. The Bible is a religious book. Some used a textbook. It was called the *New England Primer*. Many people also read a book by Cotton Mather. He was a minister. He wrote a book about witchcraft.

Girls usually helped their mothers. They learned how to cook, clean, and sew. Many girls made a **sampler**. It is a piece of cloth with sewing on it. Girls practiced different ways to sew on a sampler. Girls' clothing came in several parts. Girls wore an armless shirt. Then they tied sleeves to the shirt. They also wore a skirt.

People spoke differently than they do today. For instance, a girl's skirt was called a *petticoat*. A boy's pants were called *breeches*. If something was backward, it was *arsy varsy*. Instead of saying "*Excuse me*," people said "*Pray, pardon me*."

Medical care was not good. There were few doctors. Even doctors did not know how to cure most illnesses. Diseases like smallpox and measles were common. Many children died at a young age. Other children lost their parents. Women died more often than men. Women had babies. Having babies was very risky back then.

Many girls made samplers. A sampler showed off sewing skills.

Old-time religion

People in Salem went to church each Sunday. They called their church a "meetinghouse." It was the center of the town's activities.

Sunday was the only day off work. It was also the best chance for people to meet with friends. Salem had no theaters. People looked to the minister of the church to give an exciting **sermon**. A sermon is a speech about religion.

People got together to talk at the meetinghouse. The **witch** trials were held there, too. This shows a meetinghouse in Massachusetts. It was like many in the 1600s.

Buildings in Salem were made of wood. Most were very simple. Everyone pitched in to build the local meetinghouse.

People in Salem did not have much money. Most of their goods served a purpose. This shows fragments of a small jug. There is also a rim of a metal plate. They were used by people who were part of the witch trials.

Bad magic, good magic

People believed that they could use magic without being a witch. For instance, most people feared crossing a black cat's path. They believed that would make bad things happen. But they also believed that a black cat's blood could cure sickness. Many black cats in Salem had nicks in their ears and tails. People cut them to get their blood.

The Devil Comes to Salem

People in Salem lived in wood homes. Most were small. Families ate and slept very close to each other. This house was owned by Rebecca Nurse. She was one of the women accused of using witchcraft.

Rebecca Nurse was 71 in 1692. She lived in this house with her husband.

The hunt for **witches** began in the home of Reverend Samuel Parris. He was a minister in Salem. In January 1692, his daughter Betty began acting strangely. She ran around. She dived under furniture. She had headaches. Doctors knew little about illness. So they blamed it on witchcraft.

Parris owned a slave named Tituba. Tituba wanted to help Betty. Some of Betty's friends joined Tituba. They made a "witch cake." It was made of grain. It was also made of Betty's urine. Tituba and the girls fed the cake to a dog. They believed the dog would tell them what evil spirit was hurting the girl.

Rev. Parris found out about this. He was angry. He beat Tituba. He beat her until she said she was a witch.

The Reverand Samuel Parris was a minister in Salem. His actions helped cause the witch trials.

The arrests begin

In February 1692, Betty Parris's friends began acting strangely. They ran around. They said they saw scary people. They fell to the ground in pain. More and more girls behaved this way.

Some people said the teenage girls just wanted attention. But the girls said **witches** were hurting them. Most people believed the girls.

Teenage girls in Salem began acting strangely.

To the Constable of Gloster.

complaint haueing bein made to us there majesties Justices
of the peace in Salem by Ebenezer Babson of Gloster against
Elizabeth Dicor wife of wm Dicor and margret prince widow of Gloster
for that they haue grieuously hurt & Torturd Elenor Babson widow &
mary Sarjent wife of wm Sarjant Jun'r of Gloster by witchcraft
& has giuen Bond to their majesties to prosecut said Complaint
to Effect These are therfore in their majesties name to require
you to Apprehend & Seize the Bodys of Eliz: Dicor wife of william
Dicor of Boston Seaman & margret prince widow of Gloster & them
bring before their majesties Justices of the peace in Salem their to be
Examined about the promisses ffor wch this shall be your warrant
Salem 3'September 1692.

Barth'r Gedney
John. Hathorne
Jonathan. Corwin,
John Higginson
Justs peace

This is an arrest warrant. An arrest warrant says that someone should be arrested. This arrest warrant is for some people accused of being witches.

Being a witch was against the **law** (rules). At first, only three grown-up women were arrested. One was Tituba. The other two were Sarah Good and Sarah Osborn. Good and Osborn said they were not witches. But Tituba said that she was one.

Tituba also said that Good and Osborn were witches. She said that Good and Osborn had flown on poles, like broomsticks. People started to blame the two women for things that had gone wrong. They blamed them for animals that had died. They blamed them for food that had gone bad. People believed Tituba and the teenage girls. They believed Sarah Good and Sarah Osborn were witches.

15

law   rule that is made by the leaders of a place

Some people doubted the teenage girls. But others believed them. They saw the girls' strange behavior as proof that witches were attacking them.

"Are you a witch?"

More and more people were arrested for witchcraft. They were both men and women. These people told others that they were not **witches**. But even old friends called them liars. People believed the group of teenage girls who were naming witches.

Those accused of witchcraft had to go before **judges**. The judges decided who broke the **law** (rules) by being a witch. The judges held a **trial**. During a trial, the judges heard from **witnesses**. Witnesses said they had seen the accused act like witches. Judges then decided if the law had been broken.

judge	someone who decides if a person has broken the law
trial	time when judges hear from witnesses in order to make their decisions
witness	person at a trial who claims to have seen something

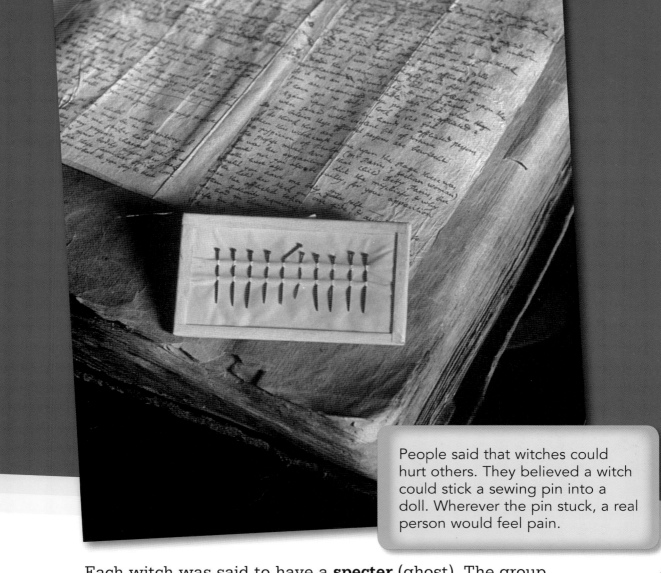

People said that witches could hurt others. They believed a witch could stick a sewing pin into a doll. Wherever the pin stuck, a real person would feel pain.

Each witch was said to have a **specter** (ghost). The group of teenage girls blamed these specters for doing bad things around Salem. People believed a specter could kill a cow. They believed it could start a fire.

People also believed that witches had "the Devil's mark." It was a wart or something odd on their skin. The judges poked these marks with pins. The person's reaction was supposed to tell whether it was a Devil's mark.

Life in jail

People accused of witchcraft were put in the Salem jail. Life there was terrible. It was dirty. There were rats and bugs. People had no heat in winter. They were boiling hot in summer. The accused **witches** were fed very badly. They had to wear chains. At least five people died in jail.

Some people called the teenage girls liars. When they did, the girls said that invisible spirits were attacking them. People saw this as proof that the girls were telling the truth.

The Salem jail was cramped and dirty. Accused witches were not able to exercise or see the outside. People died in jail. Others had health problems later on.

People back then had to pay to stay in jail. They had to pay for their own food. They even had to pay for their own chains! These same people lost everything they owned. The town leaders took their belongings. People thought it was all right to take things from witches.

The four-year-old witch

Dorcas Good was the youngest person jailed. She was the four-year-old daughter of Sarah Good. Dorcas was accused of sending her ghost to bite and choke others. Dorcas spent several months in jail. Dorcas would "cry her heart out, and go insane." She had mental problems the rest of her life.

Confess!

The **Bible** says "You shall not let a **witch** live." People in Massachusetts took that seriously. If judges said someone was a witch, that person must die. Witches were usually hung.

There was only one way to avoid hanging. The accused person had to **confess**. They had to say "I am a witch." (Men had to say, "I am a wizard.") Many accused people did not want to confess. They did not want to say something untrue.

Some people confessed because they were **tortured**. They were caused great pain. Others confessed because they were afraid. They did not want to die. When people confessed, they had to name other witches. About 50 people confessed. This caused more people to be arrested. In all, about 150 were arrested.

Those who refused to confess were killed. They were killed by hanging. Those who did confess were allowed to live. But many felt bad that they had confessed. They felt bad about hurting others.

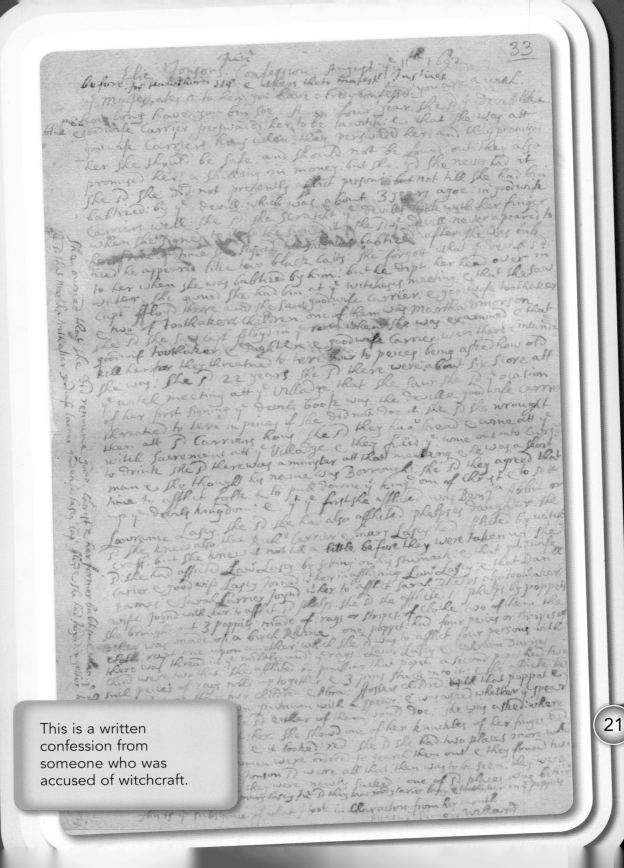

This is a written confession from someone who was accused of witchcraft.

Bridget Bishop became the first person in Salem to be hung as a witch.

Hanging witches

Bridget Bishop was accused of being a **witch**. She became the first person put to death. She was hung on June 10, 1692. Bishop was taken from the jail in an ox cart. The cart took her down the town's main street. Then she was driven to a hill outside of town. The hill has since become known as **Gallows** Hill. A gallows is a place to hang people.

Most accused witches were hung on a small hill. It soon became known as Gallows Hill.

It was a hot summer morning. A big crowd was present. Bishop's hands and feet were tied. She told the crowd that she was not a witch. Those were her last words. Then she was blindfolded. The rope was put around her neck. She was hung. Most people were glad to see her dead. They were glad that a witch had been found out. Bishop's body was buried nearby in the rocky ground. Many more accused witches would soon be buried with her.

Doubts Grow

People like Bridget Bishop and Sarah Good were not popular in Salem. But Rebecca Nurse was popular. The girls accused her of witchcraft. She was hung on July 19. Her hanging caused doubts about the **trials**. The same was true for George Burroughs. He was a former minister in Salem. Many people were angry that he was hung.

William Stoughton was the chief **judge**. He oversaw the Salem **witch** trials. He made it hard for people to defend themselves.

Giles Corey

Not everyone was hung. Giles Corey refused to be put on trial. So his punishment was more cruel. He was crushed under heavy rocks. Corey died bravely. His death made people question the witch trials, too.

The execution of George Burroughs angered many people. More and more, people saw that the witch trials were a mistake.

By the fall of 1692, the people of Salem were tired of the hangings. The teenage girls kept accusing people. But fewer people believed them. In October, the **governor** of Massachusetts stopped the trials. He was the top leader. The next May he **pardoned** those still in jail. A pardon means someone is no longer seen as a criminal. All those accused of witchcraft were released.

Apologies

Some people later said they were sorry for their role in the **witch trials**. In 1697, Samuel Sewall made his apology. He had been a **judge**. He had ordered people to their deaths. Sewall asked forgiveness for the "blame and shame of it."

That same year, Massachusetts held a **fast**. During a fast, no one can eat or drink. The fast reminded people of those who died.

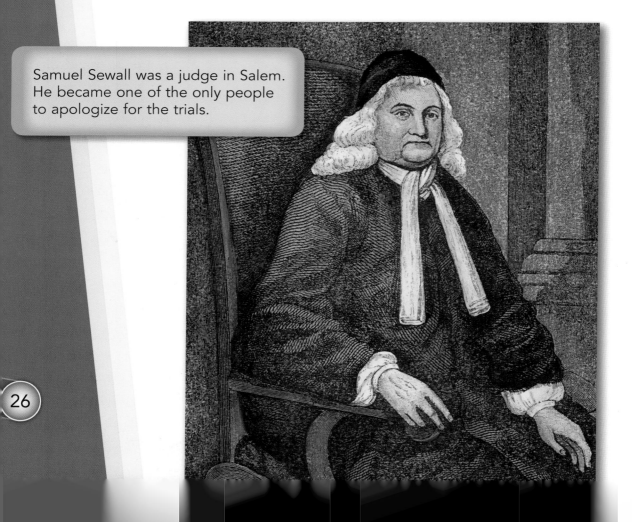

Samuel Sewall was a judge in Salem. He became one of the only people to apologize for the trials.

One of the biggest apologies came on August 25, 1706. A young woman named Ann Putnam stood up in church. As a girl, she had accused people of witchcraft. Ann **confessed**. She wrote down that she had done wrong. It was read before the church. She wrote that she believed that she had been fooled by the Devil. She begged for forgiveness.

Other people should have apologized. But they never did. Many books like these were written about the trials. They showed that the trials had been wrong.

AN
Historical ESSAY
CONCERNING
WITCHCRAFT.
WITH
OBSERVATIONS upon MATTERS OF
FACT ; tending to clear the Texts of the
Sacred Scriptures, and confute the vulgar
Errors about that Point.

AND ALSO

TWO SERMONS: One in Proof of the
Christian Religion ; The other concerning the
Good and Evil Angels.

By FRANCIS HUTCHINSON, D. D.
Chaplain in Ordinary to His Majesty, and Minister of St. *James*'s Parish in St. *Edmund's-Bury*.

PSALM XXXI. 6.
*I have hated them that hold superstitious Vanities : but
I trust in the Lord.*

1 TIM. IV. 7.
*But refuse profane and old Wives Fables, and exercise
thy self rather unto Godliness.*

LONDON:
Printed for R. KNAPLOCK, at the *Bishop's Head*, and
D. MIDWINTER, at the *Three Crowns* in St. *Paul's*
Church-yard. MDCCXVIII.

Books like this came out after the witch trials were over. They showed why the trials were wrong.

Witch City

Salem is much different today. The witch trials made Salem famous. People come to see the city. They want to see places that are tied to the **witch trials**. These visitors are called **tourists**.

Salem makes money from tourists. The tourists visit shops and museums. They spend money there. Salem now calls itself "Witch City." There is a witch on the side of police cars. Salem's high school teams are called "the Witches."

People in Salem set up this monument. It lists the names of those killed during the witch trials.

tourist   visitor who travels for pleasure

Few people believe in witches today. Instead, we see that innocent people were put to death. In 1992, Salem put up a monument. It honored the bravery of those who died.

In 1711, most of the witches were **pardoned**. That means they were found not guilty of being witches. But some were still seen as guilty. The rest were finally pardoned in 2001 on Halloween Day. The **governor** (leader) of Massachusetts said they were innocent. He signed a **law** (rule).

The witch trials made Salem famous. Today, Salem calls itself "the Witch City."

Glossary

Bible religious book

colony group of people who settle in a new land

confess when a person admits that they did something wrong

fast time when a person does not eat or drink

gallows place to hang someone

governor top leader of a colony or a state

judge someone who decides if a person has broken the law

law rule that is made by the leaders of a place

pardon statement that someone is no longer seen as a criminal

sampler piece of cloth with sewing on it

sermon a speech about religion

specter ghost

torture cause great pain

tourist visitor who travels for pleasure

trial time when judges hear from witnesses in order to make their decisions

witch female who gets evil powers from helping the Devil

witness person at a trial who claims to have seen something

wizard male who gets evil powers from helping the Devil

Want to Know More?

Books to read

Boraas, Tracey. *The Salem Witch Trials*. Mankato, Minn.: Capstone Press, 2000.

Orr, Tamra B. *People at the Center of : The Salem Witch Trials*. Chicago; Blackbirch Press, 2003.

Websites

http://www.law.umkc.edu/faculty/projects/ftrials/salem/salem.htm
The law school at the University of Missouri at Kansas City runs this helpful website on the witch trials.

http://jefferson.village.virginia.edu/salem/home.html
This University of Virginia website contains documents from the trials.

Places to visit

Salem Witch Museum
Washington Square North • Salem, MA 01970 • 978-744-1692
http://www.salemwitchmuseum.com

Rebecca Nurse Homestead
149 Pine Street • Danvers, MA 01923 • 978-774-8799
http://www.rebeccanurse.org/RNurse/AboutUs.htm

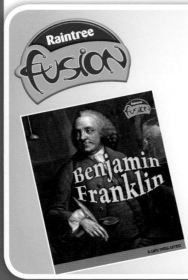

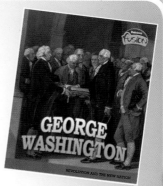

Read *George Washington: Revolution and the New Nation* to learn more about our nation's first president.

Read *Benjamin Franklin: A Life Well Lived* to learn about the many achievements of this founding father.

31

Index